GOD CARES WHEN I DO SOMETHING STUPID

BY ELSPETH CAMPBELL MURPHY
ILLUSTRATED BY JANE E. NELSON

GOD CARES WHEN I DO SOMETHING STUPID

BY ELSPETH CAMPBELL MURPHY
ILLUSTRATED BY JANE E. NELSON

Chariot Books is an imprint of David C. Cook Publishing Co., Elgin, IL 60120
GOD CARES WHEN I DO SOMETHING STUPID
© 1984 by Elspeth Campbell Murphy for the entire text and Jane E. Nelson for the illustrations
Except for brief excerpts for review purposes, no part of this book may be reproduced or used in any form without written permission from the publishers. Verses taken from the *Holy Bible: New International Version* © 1978 by the New York International Bible Society. Used by permission of the Zondervan Corporation
Printed in the United States of America
89 88 87 86   5 4 3 2
Library of Congress Cataloging in Publication Data
Murphy, Elspeth Campbell.
   God cares when I do something stupid
     (Chariot Books) (God's Word in My Heart)

  Summary: A child comes to realize that God cares about us no matter what we do.
   [1. Behavior—Fiction. 2. Christian life—Fiction]
I. Nelson, Jane E., ill   II. Title.   III. Series:
Murphy, Elspeth Campbell. God's word in my heart.
PZ7.M95316Gg   1984   [E]   83-72504
ISBN 0-89191-792-6

We are having a family reunion today.
I couldn't wait to play with my cousin who's the same age as me.
I hadn't seen him in a whole year.

Right away my cousin and I
started playing on the slide.
We made up all these ways to slide down.

First my cousin slid down on his stomach.
Then I slid down with my feet hanging over the sides.
We were going to slide down backwards,
but my grandmother made us stop.
"Be careful, or you'll get hurt," she said.

We decided to play on the swings.
My cousin raced me, and he won.
I pumped really hard to see if I could
go higher than my cousin.

I pumped so hard, I thought I would sail.
right off the swing!
And one of our tattletale baby cousins said,
"Grandma, those boys better be careful,
or they'll get hurt!"

Then I raced my cousin to the teeter-totter.
He sat down hard on one end
and wouldn't let me down.
So I pretended to be scared.
I screamed and screamed.

My aunt made him let me down.
And my mother said to us,
"Be careful, or you'll get hurt."

At lunch my cousin and I
raced to see who could eat the most.
I ate two and a half hot dogs
and seven roasted marshmallows.

My cousin ate two hot dogs
and nine roasted marshmallows.
"Slow down!" my father said.
"Don't rush! Don't gulp!"

After lunch my cousin and I started wrestling.
We were squealing because we were laughing so hard.
My mother said, "Be careful, or you'll get hurt."
We said, "We're just playing."
And she said, "You'll be fighting in a minute."
But we said, "No, we won't."

But then we sort of started fighting.
I pushed my cousin,
and he tripped over a sticking-up root
and landed on his arm!

My cousin tried to move his arm,
but he couldn't.
My aunt said she was afraid it might be broken.
I never felt so terrible in my whole life, God!
I wanted to disappear.
I wanted to crawl in a hole and hide.

Then my father came over.
At first I thought he was going to yell at me,
but he didn't.
Instead he sat down beside me
and put his arm around me.
His arm felt cozy on my shoulders.
"You look like you could use some company," he said.

"I didn't mean to hurt him," I said.
And I started to cry because I felt so awful.
"I know you didn't," Dad said softly.
"I feel so *stupid*!" I said.
Dad laughed to himself. "Believe me, Son. I know the feeling! We all get really disgusted with ourselves sometimes."

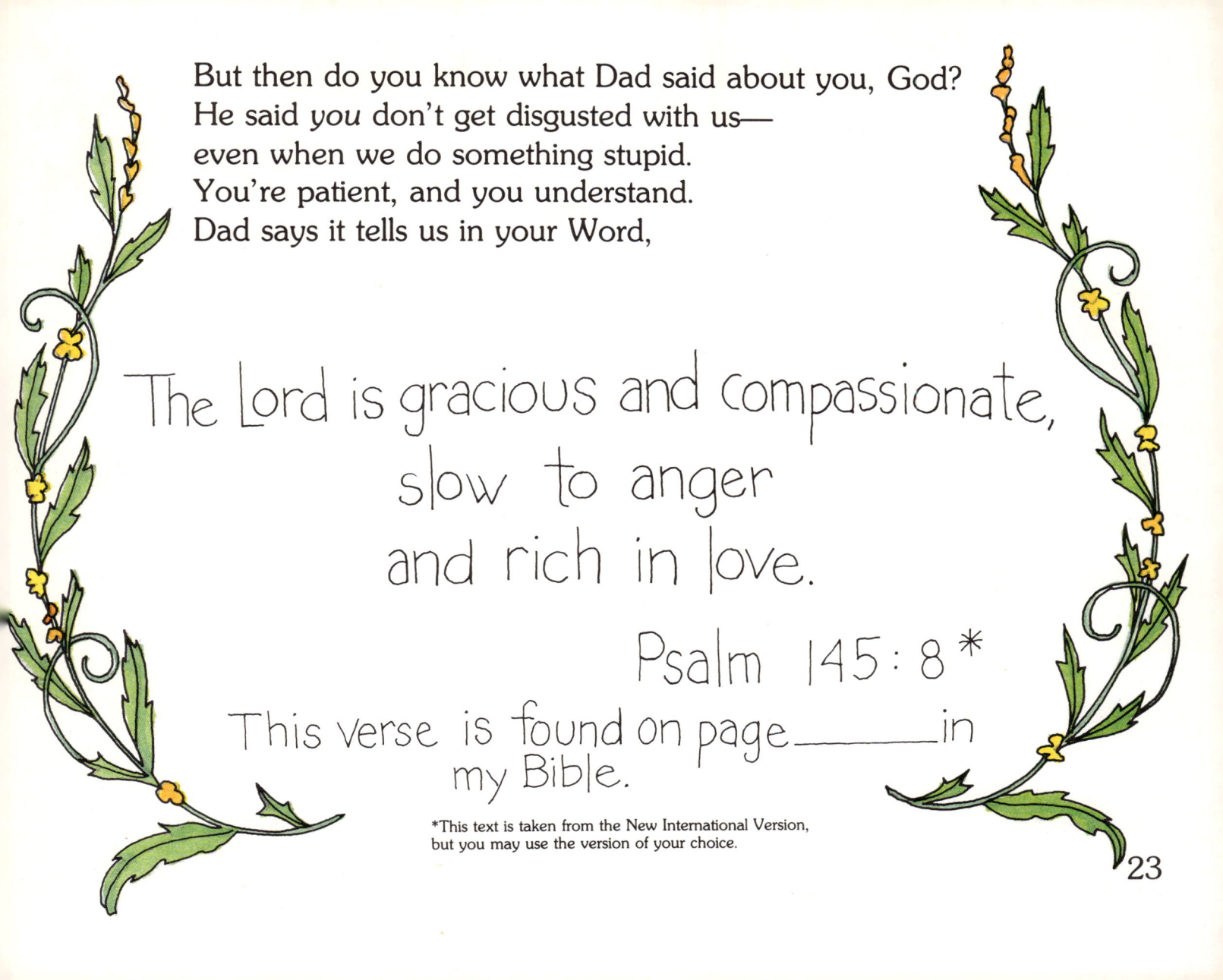

But then do you know what Dad said about you, God?
He said *you* don't get disgusted with us—
even when we do something stupid.
You're patient, and you understand.
Dad says it tells us in your Word,

The Lord is gracious and compassionate,
slow to anger
and rich in love.

Psalm 145:8*

This verse is found on page _____ in my Bible.

*This text is taken from the New International Version, but you may use the version of your choice.

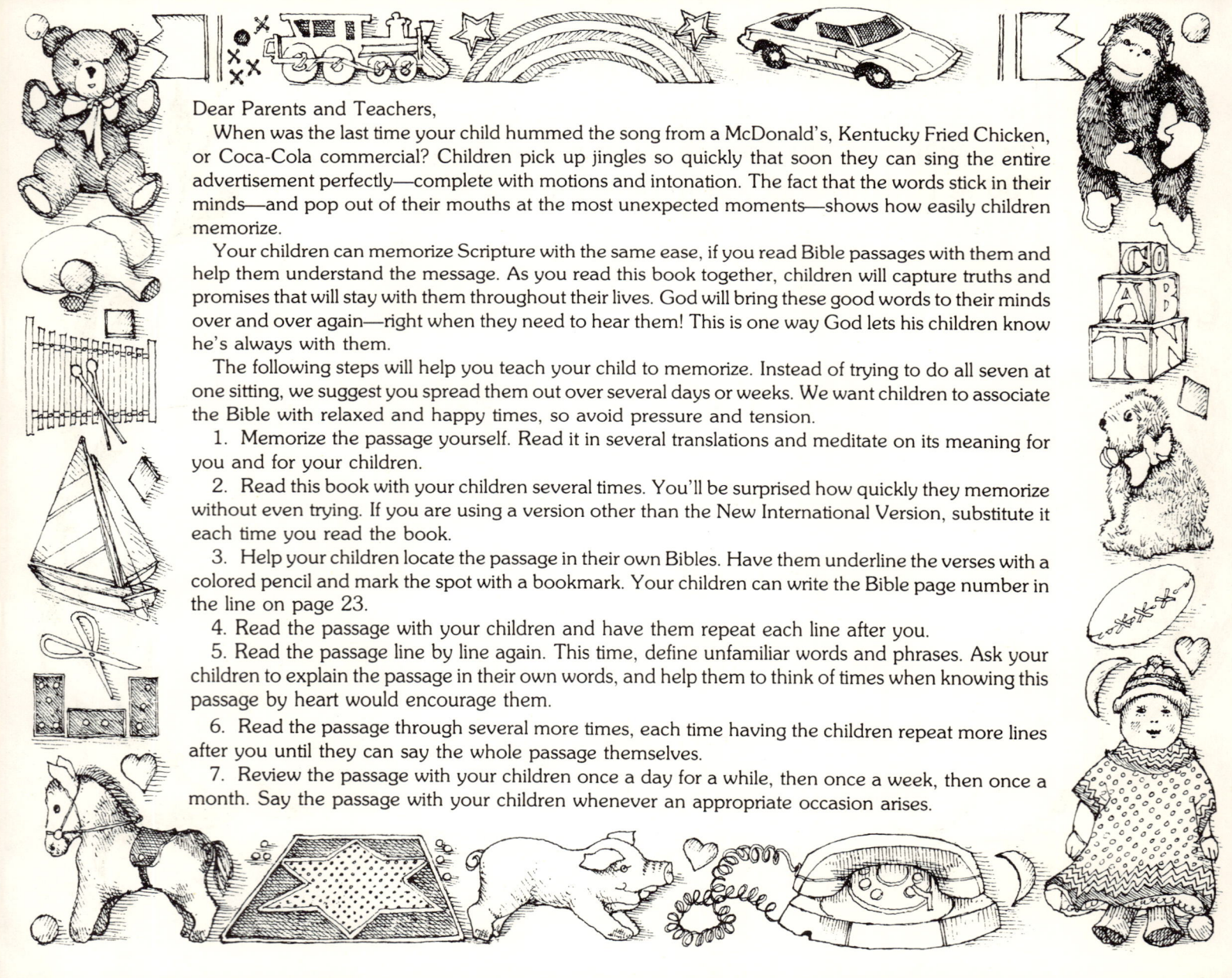

Dear Parents and Teachers,

When was the last time your child hummed the song from a McDonald's, Kentucky Fried Chicken, or Coca-Cola commercial? Children pick up jingles so quickly that soon they can sing the entire advertisement perfectly—complete with motions and intonation. The fact that the words stick in their minds—and pop out of their mouths at the most unexpected moments—shows how easily children memorize.

Your children can memorize Scripture with the same ease, if you read Bible passages with them and help them understand the message. As you read this book together, children will capture truths and promises that will stay with them throughout their lives. God will bring these good words to their minds over and over again—right when they need to hear them! This is one way God lets his children know he's always with them.

The following steps will help you teach your child to memorize. Instead of trying to do all seven at one sitting, we suggest you spread them out over several days or weeks. We want children to associate the Bible with relaxed and happy times, so avoid pressure and tension.

1. Memorize the passage yourself. Read it in several translations and meditate on its meaning for you and for your children.

2. Read this book with your children several times. You'll be surprised how quickly they memorize without even trying. If you are using a version other than the New International Version, substitute it each time you read the book.

3. Help your children locate the passage in their own Bibles. Have them underline the verses with a colored pencil and mark the spot with a bookmark. Your children can write the Bible page number in the line on page 23.

4. Read the passage with your children and have them repeat each line after you.

5. Read the passage line by line again. This time, define unfamiliar words and phrases. Ask your children to explain the passage in their own words, and help them to think of times when knowing this passage by heart would encourage them.

6. Read the passage through several more times, each time having the children repeat more lines after you until they can say the whole passage themselves.

7. Review the passage with your children once a day for a while, then once a week, then once a month. Say the passage with your children whenever an appropriate occasion arises.